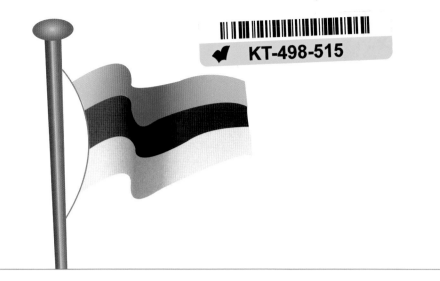

New EU Countries and Citizens

Estonia

Piret Hiisjärv
Ene Hiiepuu

A Cherrytree Book

This edition published in 2006 by Evans Brothers Limited
2A Portman Mansions
Chiltern Street
London W1U 6NR, UK

Reprinted 2006
Published by arrangement with KIT Publishers – The Netherlands

British Library Cataloguing-in-Publication Data
Hiisjarv, Piret
Estonia. - (New EU countries and citizens)
1. Estonia - Juvenile literature
I. Title
II. Hiiepuu, Ene
947.9'8
ISBN 1842343211
9781842343210

Text: Piret Hiisjärv and Ene Hiiepuu
Photographs: Jan Willem Bultje
UK editing: Sonya Newland
Design and Layout: Grafisch Ontwerpbureau Agaatsz BNO, Meppel, The Netherlands
Cover: Big Blu Ltd
Cartography: Armand Haye, Amsterdam, The Netherlands
Production: J & P Far East Productions, Soest, The Netherlands

Contents

Introduction

The Republic of Estonia is situated in north-central Europe, one of the Baltic states along the coast of the Baltic Sea. Estonia borders the Gulf of Finland in the north, Russia in the east, Latvia in the south, the Gulf of Riga in the south-west, and the Baltic Sea in the west.

Estonia also includes several hundred small islands off the coast. Although the country lies in a northerly position in Europe, it is quite mild because so much of it is bordered by the sea, which moderates the climate, keeping it relatively mild in coastal regions. Much of the interior landscape is lowland, and is characterised by many lakes that were left over from the last Ice Age.

Estonian language and culture is closely linked to Scandinavia, but its history has been more closely intertwined with Russia, despite being ruled by Germans, Swedes and Danes at different times. In 1721 Estonia came under Russian rule, and except for a brief period of independence between the two world wars, it remained so until the 1990s. The Russian influence can still be felt all over the country, and thousands of Russian people live in Estonia.

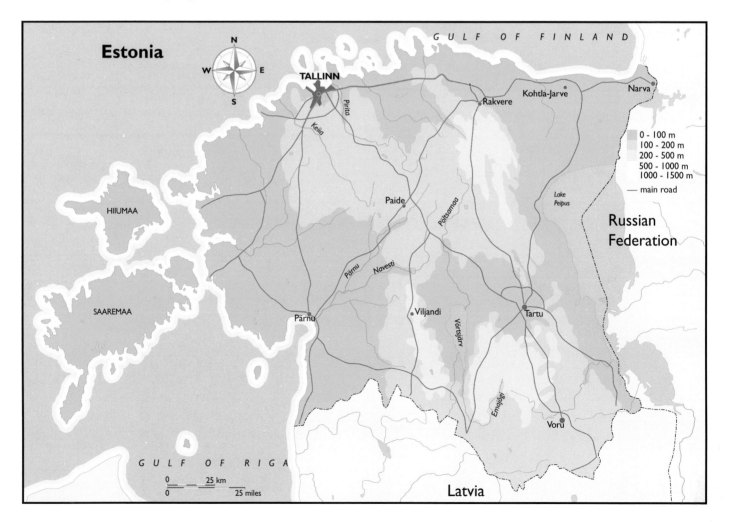

Estonia was granted full independence in 1991, one of the first countries to declare its freedom after the collapse of the Soviet communist regime, and since then it has been rebuilding its economy and other infrastructures that had suffered during the years of foreign rule. A constitution was established in 1992, in which Estonia became a parliamentary republic, governed from the capital Tallinn.

Independence has allowed the Estonian people to revive many ancient traditions that had been suppressed for centuries, and today they celebrate their heritage with great enthusiasm, in the use of their own language, the staging of festivals and the resurgence of many old customs.

Over the past decade, Estonia has concentrated on strengthening international relations by joining several organisations, including the United Nations, the World Trade Organization and UNESCO. It became a full member of the European Union in May 2004, and this has provided the country with much support in the processes of stabilising and restructuring.

▲ *There are thousands of lakes and ponds in Estonia.*

▼ *Large parts of Estonia are given over to agriculture, and this remains an important industry. Fields of rye like this one are interspersed with cornflowers – one of Estonia's national symbols.*

History

The first people to inhabit Estonia arrived there about 10,000 years ago, and the earliest proper settlement grew up in the western part of the country around 7500 BC. However, the ancestors of present-day Estonians are believed to have been hunters who arrived from parts of northern Europe between 3000 and 2000 BC.

▼ *The ancient Estonians buried their dead in stone coffins that were covered with limestone plates and surrounded by circular stone walls. Some of these graves can still be seen today at Jõelähtme, near Tallinn.*

At that time, Estonian territory was covered with forests and swamps, and the ancient peoples founded small communities around lakes and along river banks. The men hunted wild animals and fished, while the women picked berries and whatever else the forests offered. They made tools out of stones, bones and wood. Later, merchants from neighbouring lands ventured into the territory and taught the people how to process metal, so they began making tools from bronze. Gradually, raising livestock became an increasingly common way of earning a living and providing food.

► A citadel was a fortified town built on a hill or a swamp island. Its inner courtyard was surrounded by a high mound and strong wooden walls. Later, stone was used instead of wood. This is the fortress of Rakvere in northern Estonia.

By the first century BC, the use of bronze in tool- and weapon-making had given way to iron, which was much stronger and more durable. Iron tools made it easier to cut down trees for wood and to cultivate farmland. Ploughing the land and growing crops became widespread practices, and more and more people settled in one place. Gradually small villages expanded to form parishes and parishes joined to form counties. The Estonian people were good at handicrafts, and they made everything they needed, from buildings to tools and clothes.

Throughout this time the Estonians had largely lived in peace, without being threatened by invasion and conquest. However, by the sixth century increasing numbers of foreigners were entering the territory, particularly the Slavs and Vikings. The Estonians started building fortified strongholds and citadels to protect themselves from invaders. Despite threats from some regions, the Estonians built up good trading relationships with their neighbours. Merchants exchanged materials such as salt, iron, amber and tools for flax, honey, animal skins, grain and wax.

The Christian crusades

By the end of the twelfth century, most European nations had converted to Christianity, and the people of Finland and the Baltic states, including Estonia, were the only ones still following pagan rituals and beliefs. The pope organised a crusade with the aim of bringing Christianity to the Baltic nations. The crusades lasted from 1208 to 1227, and during this time the Estonians were treated harshly and forced to adopt Christianity against their will. One result of the campaign was that the Baltic lands were divided between German crusaders and Danish invaders. In some areas, small independent principalities were formed, including Livonia, which covered most of Estonia. The conquered countries were dedicated to the Virgin Mary, and Estonia is still sometimes referred to as 'Mary's Land' (Maarjamaa).

The ancient Estonians believed that every animal, bird, tree, stone and plant had a soul. They thought that fairies lived in houses and mermaids inhabited the water. Water from fresh springs flowing from the earth was believed to have healing properties. Fire had a cleansing purpose – the people believed that light from a bonfire would scare away evil forces, especially at the times of equinoxes, when day and night are of equal length. Even today, Estonians maintain the tradition of jumping over a bonfire during the autumn equinox.

◀ In the Middle Ages, Livonia had several key towns, all of which were surrounded by high walls, had very narrow streets and multi-storey buildings. Of all the medieval towns in Estonia, the capital Tallinn is the best-preserved, with many churches, a town hall and merchants' courtyards.

The Middle Ages

By the Middle Ages people of several nationalities were living in Estonian territories. The Germans were the most powerful, and made up the land-owning classes, the clergy and important town citizens. There were also some Russian merchants in the towns and cities. Livonian towns belonged to the powerful political Hanseatic League, and a lot of trade took place between Livonia and Russia. The native Estonians lived as peasants, working for powerful landlords. A landlord's property was divided into two sections. Part was 'manor land', where the peasants worked for the lord of the manor for a certain number of days each year, using their own tools and animals. The second part was farmland, which was rented to peasants for their own use. Some of the harvest was paid to the landlord as rent.

▶ Many stone churches, castles and citadels for different monastic orders were built in the countryside. The Padise monastery was constructed between 1305 and 1317, and has been destroyed and rebuilt several times during the course of its history.

The Estonian peasants had hardly any rights in the Middle Ages. They were serfs – the lowest social class – until the sixteenth century, and were not even allowed to leave their houses without the permission of their landlord.

During this time, Estonian lands were the site of several conflicts. Polish and Swedish troops occupied the country during the Livonian War (1558–83), after which Sweden gained control of Estonia. In the Great Northern War (1700–21), Estonia was invaded by Russia. This marked the beginning of the rule of the Russian tsars, which lasted for 200 years.

Although they were still ruled by foreigners, this period marked a change in fortunes for the Estonian people. In the time of Swedish rule a network of public schools was established, providing basic education and training for farmers. King Gustav Adolf II founded the University of Tartu in south-east Estonia in 1632; this was the first institute for higher education in the country, although most students were German, Swedish or Finnish.

▼ *The University of Tartu is the oldest institute of higher education in Estonia, dating from the seventeenth century.*

◀ *At the open-air museum near Tallinn, many old houses and farmhouses have been preserved and can be seen as they would have looked in medieval times.*

Life was still not easy for the Estonians. Until the end of the nineteenth century, most of them lived in the barns and sheds where grain was threshed and stored. These were made of pine wood, clay and stone, with hay or reed roofs. Country houses looked a lot like normal farms. Towards the end of the eighteenth century, landowners started developing rural estates, copying the styles they had seen during travels abroad. These estates were often surrounded by parks which contained pavilions and artificial lakes.

National awakening

Throughout these years of oppression, the Estonians always remembered their own heritage, and were determined that one day they would regain the land they had lost. At the beginning of the nineteenth century many farmers rebelled against their landlords, and in 1819 serfdom was abolished. By the middle of the century Estonian people were allowed to buy their own houses – the national awakening that would eventually lead to independence had begun.

In the nineteenth century, efforts were being made to increase knowledge of the Bible, and in Estonia this resulted in a rise in literacy amongst the population. New schools were established and books were printed. Even farmers were allowed to receive an education. The first Estonian to graduate was Friedrich Robert Faehlmann, author of the epic poem *Kalevipoeg*.

▶ *The Vanemuine was the first theatre to open in Estonia, in 1865.*

The first Estonian national weekly magazine was published in 1857. In 1865, the first amateur theatre was established, the Vanemuine. In time, this developed into a professional theatre, performing pieces in the Estonian language. By 1880, 85 per cent of the population was literate. However, the same year, the Russians began to assert their authority over the Baltic states and Russian became the official language in all schools. Despite this, the Estonians maintained and strengthened their national customs.

The National Movement gained momentum in the early years of the twentieth century. The Russian Revolution in 1917 provided Estonia and the other Baltic countries with an opportunity to seize independence and the following year the Republic of Estonia was created. It was formally established by the Tartu Peace Treaty in 1920. For the next 20 years, Estonia enjoyed a rapidly growing economy and a great surge in national culture.

▼ *The magnificent house on the Palmse estate, where the noble family Von der Pahlen lived. Palmse shows how very different the lives of the foreign ruling classes were from those of the Estonian peasant farmers.*

NICHTANGRIFSVERTRAG ZWISCHEN DEUTSCHLAND UND
DER UNION DER SOZIALISTISCHEN SOWJETREPUBLIKEN.

Die Deutsche Reichsregierung und

die Regierung der Union der Sozialistischen
Sowjetrepubliken

geleitet von dem Wunsche die Sache des Friedens
zwischen Deutschland und der UdSSR zu festigen und aus-
gehend von den grundlegenden Bestimmungen des Neutrali-
tätsvertrages, der im April 1926 zwischen Deutschland
und der UdSSR geschlossen wurde, sind zu nachstehender
Vereinbarung gelangt:

Artikel I.

Die beiden Vertragschliessenden Teile verpflich-
ten sich, sich jeden Gewaltakte, jeder agressiven Hand-
lung und jedes Angriffe gegen einander, und zwar sowohl
einzeln als auch gemeinsam mit anderen Mächten, zu ent-
halten.

Artikel II.

Falls einer der Vertragschliessenden Teile Gegen-
stand krigerischer Handlungen seitens einer dritten Macht
werden sollte, wird der andere Vertragschliessende Teil
in keiner Form diese dritte Macht unterstützen.

Artikel III.

Die Regierungen der beiden Vertragschliessenden
Teile werden künftig fortlaufend zwecks Konsultation in

F110048

▲ *The articles of the Molotov-Ribbentrop Pact, a non-aggression treaty between Germany and the Soviet Union, in which they agreed ownership of other lands. By the terms of the treaty, Estonia fell to the Soviets.*

Independence

The Soviets ruled Estonia for the next four decades. As the 1980s drew to a close, barriers between the communist East and the democratic West were being broken down all over Europe. On 23 August 1989, two million people formed a human chain stretching more than 600 km, from Tallinn in Estonia to Vilnius in Lithuania, to demonstrate against Soviet rule. The following year Estonia declared its independence from the USSR and in 1991 it became a free republic.

The Second World War

The Second World War began in 1939. Germany and the Soviet Union signed an agreement – the Molotov-Ribbentrop Pact – in which Estonia fell under the rule of the Soviets. In 1940, Soviet troops marched into and occupied Estonia, claiming that the country had 'voluntarily' agreed to become a state in the Soviet Union. More than 60,000 Estonians were deported or killed in the first year of Soviet occupation.

In 1941, the Germans went back on their word and invaded the Baltic countries. Many Estonians saw the German troops as liberators from the Soviet regime and fought on their side during the invasion. For the next three years Estonia was ruled by Germany, and it was only in 1944 that the Soviets reoccupied Estonia. Their revenge on the local people was harsh, and many Estonians fled abroad. Those that remained were forced to give up their land and livestock, and all businesses fell under Soviet state control. Russian was declared the official language once again.

The Soviet government established an industrial network that attracted many Russians to Estonia. The number of natives in the country continued to decline after the war ended in 1945 and by 1989 only 61.5 per cent of the population was Estonian.

▼ *In 1988 more than 100,000 people gathered at a festival to sing patriotic songs and to show the world how much they wanted to be an independent nation. It was known as the 'Singing Revolution'.*

The country

Estonia is a small country, just 45,226 km², including the islands offshore in the Baltic Sea. The largest of these are Saaremaa and Hiiumaa. The country is around 240 km from north to south and 350 km from east to west. The landscape is characterised by marshy lowlands; it is mostly flat in the north, and more hilly in the south. The Baltic coastline stretches for 3,794 km.

Estonia is a rather low and featureless country. The highest points are not much more than 200 metres above sea level. Despite this, the countryside is diverse. Large forests, open swamps and marshes, fields, meadows and hills alternate with lowlands, valleys and hollows. Almost half of Estonia is covered with forests, many of them very old, and the Estonian forest reserve is one of the largest in Europe.

Lakes and rivers

There are some 1,400 lakes in Estonia. The largest is Lake Peipsi, which has a surface area of 3,600 km². Peipsi is the fourth-largest lake in Europe. There are more than 7,000 rivers and streams, but only nine of them are longer than 100 km. The longest is the Pärnu River, which stretches 144 km across the country.

▼ *The coast in Lahemaa National Park in the north of the country, bordering the Baltic Sea.*

Enelin is talking about a class trip he made to northern Estonia. 'I saw a big pile of stones and I wondered how it had been created. I asked my teacher and she told me to find a stone from the beach and then to throw it on to the pile while making a wish. I realised that the pile was made up of wishing stones that people had thrown there over the years.'

▼ *The Jägala waterfall, in northern Estonia, is the most powerful in the country. The water falls from a height of 7.8 metres.*

Regions

Although Estonia is a rather flat country, its natural environment varies across the different regions. Northern Estonia is characterised by shoals – peninsulas that reach far into the sea, creating bays and inlets. In some places the coastal area is gently sloping, in others it rises like a high terrace straight up from the coastline.

▶ *The Emajõgi River is unique because it does not flow into the sea like the other rivers. Instead it flows into lakes Vortjarv and Peipsi.*

Southern Estonia has the highest hills in the country. Suur Munamägi ('Big Egg Mountain'), which is 318 metres high, is the highest hill in the Baltic states. The domed landscape of southern Estonia is interspersed with a number of rivers and small lakes. Southern Estonia also contains the deepest lake – Rõuge Suurjärv (38 metres deep) – and the longest navigable river in Estonia – the Emajõgi. One of the biggest attractions in southern Estonia is the Piusa caves. These are man-made caves that used to be used for sandstone mining.

▲ *One of the many lakes in southern Estonia.*

▼ *The Piusa caves, hidden in this sand quarry, are home to a colourful pillar maze which is almost 4 metres high. This is one of the largest hibernation areas for bats in Northern Europe.*

A traditional Estonian folktale tells of the birth of the Emajõgi River. When Grandfather created the world it was a good place to live, but soon the animals were fighting with one another. Grandfather called all the animals together and said: 'I can see that you need a king who will control you. To welcome him you must dig a deep, wide river into which all other rivers can flow. The name of the river will be Emajõgi.' The animals did as grandfather told them, and he poured water into the river, gave it life with his breath and determined its course. This is how Emajõgi was created.

▲ *It is not unusual for the first snow to fall in September, but this usually melts quite quickly.*

Western Estonia is a particularly low, flat region; the land is typically about 20 metres above sea level and the coastline is very ragged. The country's best-known conservation area lies in Matsalu, in western Estonia. This is an important nesting and migration place for waterfowl. Saaremaa and Hiiumaa, the country's largest islands, are also situated in western Estonia. The islands are characterised by pastures with junipers, shingled coastal areas, well-preserved old houses with stone fences and thatched roofs, and windmills. The people who live on the islands observe many old customs. They wear their own traditional costumes and they speak in a dialect of the Estonian language. Several islands, including the island of Kihnu, are on the UNESCO World Heritage list.

Climate

Estonia has a moderate climate, which is influenced by its situation on the Baltic Sea. The country is relatively damp, cool and windy, and it can experience sudden and considerable changes in the weather. Winters are wet and summers are quite warm, although the heat never gets unbearable. Because Estonia is quite far north, winter days are short, only six hours, but in the summer, the days are long – up to 18 hours.

The summer months in Estonia are June, July and August. The weather is warm enough to sunbathe on the beaches or to swim in the lakes or sea. In July the average temperature in Estonia is 18°C and the waters can reach temperatures of 22°C.

▶ *Late summer and early autumn are particularly beautiful in Estonia, as the forests and bogs become cascades of colour.*

Mart is sledging with his friends. 'While the snow is slowly melting, we like to make snowmen, statues and castles out of snow. We have snowball fights,' he explains. 'Winter is fun in Estonia, because we can go skiing, skating and sledging.'

Autumn begins in September. The temperature drops, and the forests and plants in the boggy areas are turned into a riot of colour. Snow arrives early in Estonia, sometimes even in September. However, this first snowfall does not last long. The proper winter season begins in December, and from then until February snow covers the ground. The temperatures in winter can be very changeable – from 3°C to -25°C.

▼ *The first spring flowers are usually snowdrops, which appear in late February or March.*

The spring months – March, April and May – bring a mixture of rain and sun. The inner mainland warms up faster than the sea, so the coastal areas are not as warm in spring as the rest of Estonia. However, during the summer months the humidity in coastal regions is higher than it is inland, and it therefore feels warmer.

Estonia is quite a wet country, and even during the summer there can be sudden downpours. In fact, the heaviest rainfall is in August. The average annual rainfall is 500–700 mm.

Towns and cities

Estonia is a small country and only two of its cities have populations of more than 100,000 – Tallinn and Tartu. Despite this, 70 per cent of the Estonian population lives in the towns and cities. The main cities are located close to the Baltic coastline; further inland there are mainly small towns and villages.

▼ *The first written references to Tallinn date from 1154, and many medieval monuments can still be seen in the city.*

▲ *The Kadriorg Palace was founded by Russian Tsar Peter I. Today it houses the Estonian Art Museum's foreign collection.*

Tallinn

Tallinn is the capital of Estonia and its largest city, with around 500,000 inhabitants. This is the political and cultural heart of the country, where the government buildings and embassies are located, as well as theatres, museums and many old religious buildings.

The town hall in Tallinn was built in the fourteenth century.

Tallinn is situated on the Gulf of Finland, and there has been a settlement here since at least the twelfth century. In 1219 Waldemar II of Denmark destroyed the existing town and built a fortress there. The name Tallinn comes from the Estonian *Taani linn*, which means 'Danish castle'. Many historical buildings survive in Tallinn, including the thirteenth-century Gothic church of St Olai and the town hall.

Today the city is a major Baltic port and a key industrial centre for shipbuilding, manufacturing, metalworking and food processing.

▼ *Tartu Town Hall.*

Tartu

Tartu is the second-largest city in Estonia, with 105,000 inhabitants. Situated in south-eastern Estonia on the Emajõgi River, this is the oldest town in the Baltic, founded in 1030. It is home to Tartu University, established in 1632 by Gustav Adolf II of Sweden and one of the oldest universities in Northern Europe. The oldest theatre in Estonia, the Vanemuine (see page 11), can also be found here, as well as the Estonian National Museum.

◀ Fort Ivangorod stands on the Russian side of the Narva River, overlooking the town of Narva.

Narva

Narva has around 67,000 inhabitants and lies on the border with Russia, on the banks of the Narva River. Narva was founded by the Danes in 1223 and fell to the Livonian Knights in 1346. Two fortresses stand on the banks of the Narva – Fort Ivangorod was built by Ivan III of Russia to face the Hermann Fortress built by the knights on the opposite bank.

The first battle of the Great Northern War (see page 9) was fought at Narva between the Swedes and the Russians. The Swedes won, but the town was recaptured in 1704, and remained under Russian rule until 1919.

Today the town is a leading textile centre and producer of electric power. There are several other industries in Narva, including sawmills, flax and food-processing factories.

◀ The fifteenth-century Hermann Fortress, built by the German Livonian Knights, with its 50-metre tower.

Pärnu

Pärnu is the fourth-largest town in Estonia, with around 44,000 inhabitants. It is situated in the south-west of the country on the Gulf of Riga, and is widely known as the summer capital of Estonia because of its parks, white-sand beaches and recreation centres.

The town was founded around 1250 by the Livonian Knights, and was part of the Hanseatic League. After the order of knights was dissolved in the sixteenth century, Pärnu was fought over by Sweden, Russia and Poland; it was reincorporated into Estonia in 1918.

▶ The seaport Pärnu is a beach and health resort.

Otepää

Otepää is said to be the winter capital of Estonia because there is a great deal of snow there in the winter, which attracts skiers and other winter-sports enthusiasts. It hosts the popular annual ski marathon.

The town is situated on the shores of Lake Pühajärve ('Holy Lake'), about an hour's travel south from Tartu. It was first mentioned in written documents dating from 1116, when a fortress was built here and, like many Estonian towns, it suffered during the struggles between foreigners for rule of the region. During the Great Northern War the entire area surrounding Otepää was devastated, and during the Second World War most of the town was razed to the ground by German and Russian troops.

▲ *The wooden station in Haapsalu is now a railway museum.*

Health resorts

Haapsalu is a seaside town in western Estonia. It has long been known for its warm sea waters and mud, which are believed to have health-giving properties. It became a popular health resort during the period of Russian rule, and it still attracts many visitors today.

Kuressaare is another major health resort, on the largest Estonian island Saaremaa. It has a well-preserved old town with narrow streets and small squares. People come here for the beaches and the health-giving mud treatments

▶ *The Bishop's Castle in Kuressaare, dating from the fourteenth century.*

People and culture

There are around 1.3 million people living in Estonia, but only 68 per cent of them are Estonians. The largest minority group is Russian (26 per cent). Other ethnic groups living in Estonia include Ukrainians, Belarusians, Finns, Latvians, Poles, Lithuanians and Germans.

The high number of Russians living in Estonia is due to the fact that until the 1990s, Estonia was under the rule of the Soviet Union. One of the most controversial decisions made after independence was limiting citizenship in the country to ethnic Estonians, which meant that inhabitants from other groups were denied many civil rights. This particularly affected the thousands of Russians living in Estonia, who were declared foreigners in 1993.

Estonia has a low population density – only 32 people per square kilometre, and a high proportion of these (70 per cent) live in the major towns and cities.

Language

Estonian belongs to the Finno-Ugric family of languages, which also includes Finnish and Hungarian. There are believed to be as many as one million Estonian speakers all over the world. The language has no relationship to those of the other Baltic counties, Latvia and Lithuania. Although Estonian is the country's official language, 35 per cent of the population speaks Russian.

Estonian uses the Latin alphabet, but some letters can be used with or without accents to indicate what kind of sound they make. A variety of dialects are still spoken in different regions. Most young people can also speak a little English.

▼ *The largest towns and cities, which lie around the edge of Estonia, are home to the majority of the country's population.*

▼ Postimees (*'The Courier'*) *has the widest circulation of any Estonian daily newspaper. Several English-language newspapers are also available in Estonia, including* The Baltic Times *and the* Tallinn City Paper.

◀ *A view across Tallinn shows the church spires, including that of the Lutheran Cathedral. Several different religions exist side by side in Estonia.*

Religion

Many different faiths are followed in Estonia, and the constitution itself states that everyone has freedom of conscience, religion and thought.

The most widespread religion is Lutheranism – a Protestant sect, formally established in Estonia in 1686. There are also many followers of the Russian Orthodox Church because of the large numbers of Russians living in Estonia. There is an Estonian Orthodox Church as well, which was granted rights of self-government from the Russian Church in 1993. Other denominations, such as Roman Catholics, Jews, Baptists and Methodists, are also free to worship in their own churches.

▶ *The church in Jõelähtme was built in the fourteenth century and is one of the oldest churches in Estonia.*

◀ *Arvo Pärt is the best-known contemporary Estonian composer.*

Music

The Estonians love music, and they have hosted song festivals since 1869. These are great celebrations with performances by musical companies, dance groups and different types of bands from all over Estonia. The whole nation joins together for these events.

Since 1961, Estonia has also celebrated special song and dance festivals for young people. Apart from traditional songs, they perform modern music from contemporary composers. The most famous Estonian composer is Arvo Pärt, who writes beautiful contemporary choir music. These festivals are especially for young people, and only youth orchestras, and young musicians and singers are allowed to take part.

Festivals and celebrations

Estonians celebrate Christmas in much the same way as the rest of Europe, and Santa Claus and his elves bring gifts for the children. At Easter, children paint eggs and in some families the Easter bunny hides presents under their pillows. These holidays have only officially been celebrated in the last few years. When Estonia was part of the Soviet Union, the public celebration of Christmas and Easter was forbidden.

Estonians have always celebrated special days according to the ancient traditions in their national calendar. The most popular of these is the Midsummer Day festival, celebrated on 24 June. Other popular celebrations are Kadri Day and Martinmas Day in November, when people dress up in costumes and go around singing, dancing and telling stories in exchange for sweets. People used to believe that Kadris (St Catherine) and Martinus (St Martin) would bring a good harvest. Children also enjoy Shrovetide celebrations, six weeks before Easter, when there is usually snow on the ground and they have sledging competitions.

▲ *During the Tallinn Song Festival a special stage is built. The stage can accommodate as many as 24,000 singers at one time.*

▶ *Stamps celebrating Estonian culture, showing people in traditional dress.*

Pilleriin and Tina are talking about their favourite festivals. 'Midsummer's Day is linked to the summer solstice,' explains Pilleriin. 'This is a time of beautiful white nights, when there is almost no darkness. Midsummer Night has, for years, been considered a time of wonder. According to legend, it is a time when the fern plant blossoms, and anyone who finds this blossom will become rich, wise and happy. Nowadays, those who are in love go looking for the fern blossom at dusk on Midsummer's Eve.'

Tina says: 'My favourite festivals are Martinmas and Kadri Day in November. We all disguise ourselves in costumes. On Martinmas Day we wear rags, but on Kadri Day we wear white clothes. We put on masks or paint our faces so no one will recognise us. Then we go from door to door singing and dancing, and people give us sweets as a reward.'

▲ *On Midsummer Day, people make bonfires and dance and sing around them. In ancient times people believed the fires would protect them from evil and bring a good harvest.*

Sport

Playing sport is a popular pastime in Estonia, and around 55 per cent of the population, both children and adult, takes part in some kind of sporting activity. Since independence, new sports grounds and gyms have been built and old ones have been refurbished across the country. The money spent on sports is considered to be an investment in the future.

The most popular sports are football, basketball and volleyball. There are also several important running events organised every year: the Tartu Autumn Run, the May Run for women and a Health Run. Popular sports for amateurs are skiing, swimming, canoeing and cycling. Skiing is the most popular winter sport and many Estonians attend the Tartu Ski Marathon.

Sport is one of the ways that Estonia can bring its achievements and interests to the attention of the world. Seeing the national flag being hoisted and hearing the national anthem being played in honour of an Estonian athlete is a much-prized moment.

▶ *Estonian Erki Nool celebrates winning the gold medal for the decathlon at the 2000 Olympics in Sydney.*

National symbols

Estonians take great pride in the natural beauty of their country, and certain elements have been adopted as national symbols. The chimney swallow is the national bird of Estonia. It has a bluish-black coat, kite tail and a ginger throat with white tie. It builds its nest under the eaves of houses. Estonians believe the chimney swallow brings the warm summer weather. In ancient times, they also believed the bird brought good luck.

An old Estonian tale relates the story of a slave girl who worked for a miserly old landlady. She was given too much work and not enough food to eat. The girl turned into a swallow and flew out of the window with a black scarf around her shoulders.

Siret lives on a farm in the countryside. 'We have a beautiful garden with apple, plum and pear trees, berry bushes and flowers,' she tells us. 'My parents raise farm animals. We have a pig, a flock of sheep, a cow, chickens and a rooster. We also have a vegetable garden in which we grow our own produce. My favourites are the strawberries. It's all very good for you.'

The national flower of Estonia is the cornflower. This beautiful deep blue-purple flower grows in rye fields across the country – cornflowers and rye almost always grow together. Flour is ground from rye grains, from which black bread is made. This is one of the most popular types of bread in Estonia.

▼ *The 100-crown note shows Lydia Koidula, an Estonian poet and playwright. The 25-crown note shows the writer Anton Hansen-Tammsaare.*

The flag

Even the colours on the Estonian flag are related to nature. The flag is divided into three equal horizontal bands in the national colours. The blue represents the clear sky and a firm belief in the future. The black band represents the earth, the ancient feeder of mankind. The white stands for purity and hope.

The Estonian national coat of arms depicts three blue lions, one beneath the other, surrounded by oak branches, and it is the most ancient of Estonia's national symbols. The three lions have been used since the thirteenth century, when they served as the coat of arms for Tallinn, which was then under Danish rule.

Currency

The country's currency is the Estonian crown (or kroon – EEK). There are roughly 23 crowns in one British pound, and 15 crowns to one euro. The crown is divided into 100 senti. Banknotes are available in denominations of 1, 2, 5, 10, 25, 50, 100 and 500 crowns. Coins are issued in 5, 10, 20 and 50 senti pieces, and in 1 and 5 crown pieces.

The banknotes depict famous Estonian people and symbols that Estonians relate to their country, such as the sea, Estonian villages, an oak tree and the opera house in Tallinn, amongst others.

Administration

Estonia has 15 counties, which are divided into smaller parishes. There are more than 200 parishes in Estonia. Approximately 30 per cent of Estonians live in the countryside, in smaller settlements that vary greatly in size and age. The larger settlements can be home to hundreds of people and usually have a few shops, a medical centre, a church, a school and a town hall. However, the smaller villages might only consist of a few buildings surrounded by fields. Places like this may not even have a shop, let alone a school or any other amenities. Today there are many small villages in Estonia inhabited largely by older people. Young people have moved away to larger settlements or to the towns and cities, where it is easier to study and find work.

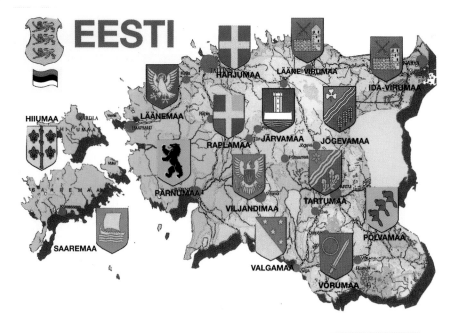

This map of Estonia shows its 15 counties. Each one has its own coat of arms.

Government

Since 28 June 1992, after 50 years of occupation by the Soviet Union, Estonia has operated as a multi-party republic, which means it is run by representatives of a number of different political parties. The constitution under which it operates was established on this date.

The parliament is called the Riigikogu. It has 101 members who are all elected by the population to serve a four-year term. The president is elected by parliament, and holds office for five years. In reality the president wields little power and major decisions are made by parliament under the leadership of the prime minister. The prime minister is chosen by the president, but has to be approved by the other members of parliament. All Estonian citizens over the age of 18 are allowed to vote in elections.

The government consists of a prime minister and a number of ministers. There is a Minister of Education and Research, a Minister of Justice, Ministers of Foreign Affairs, Home Affairs, Social Services, Defence, Environment, Culture, Agriculture, Economic Affairs, and Communication, and a Minister of Finance. The prime minister oversees the activities and portfolios of all the others.

In the most recent elections, on 2 March 2003, the Estonian Centre Party received 25.4 per cent of the votes, and the Union for the Republic (Res Republica) received 24.6 per cent. Both parties have 28 representatives in the parliament. There are six other main political parties in Estonia, including the Estonian United Russian People's Party, set up to ensure that the Russian population is represented in the running of the country. The current president (since 2001) is Arnold Rüütel. The prime minister, chosen in 2003, is Juhan Parts.

Education

Compulsory education lasts for nine years in Estonia, between the ages of seven and 16. Many children are sent to crèches before the age of three, and after this they can attend nursery schools up to the age of seven; these are usually divided into classes with children of a similar age.

▼ These nursery-school children are doing a 'newspaper dance'. Each child dances to music on a sheet of newspaper. When the music stops they have to fold the newspaper in half and carry on dancing. Those who step off the paper are out.

Compulsory education

Estonia has a single-structure education system, which means that it is not divided into different types of school until children reach the age of 16. Year 1 begins at age seven and after Year 9 pupils are allowed to leave school and get a job if they want to. However, schooling is divided into three levels: Years 1 to 3, 4 to 6 and 7 to 9. In the first two stages children are taught all subjects by one teacher. At the third level different subjects are taught by specialist teachers.

At school, children study several basic subjects, including the Estonian language, maths, geography, natural science and history. As they get older they also learn English or German from Year 3, Russian from Year 6, biology from Year 7, and physics from Year 8.

Lessons usually start at 8 o' clock in the morning and end about 2 or 3 o'clock in the afternoon. Pupils have a break for lunch, and most children eat the hot meal provided by the school. Lunches usually consist of roast meat or soup and a dessert. Younger children, in Years 1 to 4, get free lunches. Older pupils have to pay, although local authorities help to pay for school lunches for children from very large or poor families.

◀ Most schools provide a hot meal in the middle of the day.

Maret and her classmates are waiting for their teacher to arrive. They are discussing their favourite lessons – most of them enjoy physical education and creative lessons like music and art. Languages are also popular – children are taught English or German from the age of nine in Estonia.

There is a national curriculum in Estonia, which outlines which subjects must be taught and the information that must be covered within these subjects depending on what level the pupils are at. It gives guidelines for the organisation of school time – the number of hours that must be spent on compulsory and optional subjects in a school week. The curriculum also sets achievement targets for each age group. Children are taught in classes of the same age, and there can be no more than 36 students per class. If there are fewer than 20 children in a class, it may be combined with another class to make up the numbers.

School holidays

The school year lasts for just over nine months. It usually starts at the beginning of September and ends in the first week of June. Estonians call the first day of school 'wisdom day'. During the year, pupils have several holidays. They have two weeks over Christmas, and one week off for Easter. The summer holidays last for nearly three months. In addition to this, there is an autumn holiday – one week, usually at the end of October – and two public holidays, one in February and one in March.

Free time

During the holidays, or at the weekends or evenings, most children like to play outside. They spend their afternoons playing football with their friends, cycling, roller skating or skateboarding. Some children attend 'hobby clubs' in the evenings, which are often held at school. Here they might learn music, art or athletics.

▶ *School trips are often organised to places of historical interest in Estonia. These children are visiting Fort Hermann in Narva.*

◄ *Many schools now have computer rooms, or allow students access to computers in their libraries, where children can surf the Internet or research a school project.*

Pupils usually have one or two hours of homework to do in the evenings. Once this has been completed, children might watch some television or play computer games. They might look on the Internet and talk through chat rooms – sometimes to friends in other countries. At the weekends, going to the cinema is a popular pastime for young people. A cinema ticket costs the equivalent of about £5.

Higher education

After Year 9 students are allowed to leave school. However, there is also the option of going on to higher education in the form of upper secondary schools, called gymnasiums, or vocational secondary schools, where they will learn more practical subjects to train them for a particular job or profession. Courses at secondary schools last for three years.

At the age of 19, if they have a secondary-school diploma, students can apply to attend one of Estonia's universities. The most famous of these is the University of Tartu (see page 9), but there are several others, including the Concordia International University of Estonia and the Estonian Agricultural University. Tallinn is home to the Technical University and the University of Educational Sciences. In addition to these, Estonia has a number of academies, where students can specialise in subjects like music, the arts or business studies.

Cuisine

Estonians have always eaten what they grow in their fields and gardens, and they use a great deal of fresh produce in their recipes. For this reason traditional dishes depend heavily on the season. Estonian favourites include dark rye bread and dishes made from potatoes, vegetables and fish.

▼ Motley dog is a chilled cake made from biscuits, cocoa and marmalade.

Recipe for motley dog

Ingredients
400g biscuits
200g butter
4 tablespoons cocoa
100g sugar
100g diced marmalade

Mash the biscuits and then add the marmalade cubes. Melt the butter and add the sugar and cocoa. Allow the mixture to cool down and then pour it over the biscuits and marmalade. Mix and pour it on to greaseproof paper and wrap into a tube. Put it in the refrigerator and leave it there for three hours. Cut the cake into pieces before serving.

Popular dishes

In springtime, Estonian cuisine uses a lot of lamb and veal. The favourite fish of this season is perch, which can be caught in the lakes. Wild leeks and rhubarb are also characteristic of spring in Estonia. Throughout the summer, dishes are very aromatic and contain lots of herbs. New potatoes accompany many meals. By the autumn, fresh berries have been collected and these form the basis of many dishes, especially sauces and accompaniments. This is the hunting season in Estonia, and game is often caught in the forests, including boar, goat and pheasant. In winter Estonians enjoy eating meat that has been smoked to preserve it for when it cannot be bought fresh. Dishes such as 'blood sausage' are served with spicy sauerkraut (pickled cabbage). They drink mulled wine and make gingerbread.

Mushrooms

An Estonian tradition in the early autumn is gathering mushrooms, and people have done this for centuries. Families and friends gather together and take trips to the forests, where they hunt in the undergrowth for the different types of edible mushrooms that can be found there. One of the most popular mushrooms is the boletus, which has an umbrella-shaped cap. People have to be careful, though, because some species of boletus are poisonous. Other highly valued mushrooms include chanterelles and milk mushrooms. The Latin name for these is *Lactarius* and there are about 200 different species. They are called milk mushrooms because when they are squeezed or pressed they release a milky substance. Some species, like the *Lactarius deliciosus* are edible, but they don't taste very nice; they have a grainy texture and are rather sour. However, other types have much more flavour and are very popular.

▲ *Mushroom-collecting is a national pastime, and many traditional dishes use fresh mushrooms.*

Viljar is talking about her favourite foods. 'I always look forward to my birthday, when my mother makes potato salad, cooks frankfurters and bakes a cake made of biscuits,' she tells us. 'Actually I like hamburgers a lot, but my mother thinks they aren't good for you so we don't have them very often. On a normal day we eat different dishes, including potatoes with mincemeat sauce, mixed vegetables and, of course, pasta. I like mashed potatoes very much. Mother cooks the potatoes until they are very mushy, adds warm milk and diced onion and mixes all the ingredients into a sort of porridge.'

▲ *Cranberries are nicknamed 'pearls of the bog' in Estonia, because they grow in marshy areas.*

Once they have been collected, the mushrooms are used fresh in many dishes, or they are salted, dried and preserved so they can be enjoyed at other times of the year.

Berries

As well as mushrooms, people also go to the forests to hunt for wild berries in the late summer and early autumn. Blackberries, cowberries and cranberries grow in and around the bogs and marshes. Blueberries and bilberries flourish in the swamps and pine forests. Wild strawberries and raspberries grow in clearings in the forests. Once collected, these berries are made into jams and preserves, and serving them with pancakes is a favourite Estonian dish. Some people sell pots of home-made jams on street corners and in the market places.

Hazelnuts can also be found in the forests; these usually ripen around September, by which time their shells have turned brown and are easy to remove. Some people also collect fresh herbs from the forests. These are dried and used as flavourings in recipes or to make herb tea.

In Estonia, people grow half of the fruits and vegetables they need in their own gardens. They prefer to eat locally cultivated fruits and vegetables than those imported from other countries. Produce traditionally grown in private gardens includes potatoes, onions, peas, beans, carrots, pumpkins and celery, as well as dill and other herbs. Most gardens also have beds of strawberry and rhubarb plants. Other fruits include apples, plums, cherries, blackcurrants, redcurrants, raspberries and gooseberries. Many people have greenhouses in their gardens, in which they cultivate tomatoes and cucumbers.

▶ *Fruit trees are abundant in Estonia, and people who live in the country often have whole orchards of them. They gather the fruit and make jams and preserves out of it.*

Potatoes

Potatoes are abundant in Estonia. They are cultivated in large numbers on farms, but people also grow them in their gardens. They are used as an accompaniment to almost every meal and are served in different ways. Potatoes are also one of the most important products to be exported to other countries from Estonia.

Fish

Fish – like bread – is part of the staple diet of Estonian people, especially those who live in the coastal regions. Important fish caught in the sea are Baltic herring, sprat, plaice and eel. The most popular freshwater fish are perch, pike, bream, roach and smelt. A record-breaking pike was once caught in an Estonian lake – it weighed 19.9 kg and was 22 years old! Restaurants across the country offer a variety of fresh fish dishes cooked in traditional ways.

Under-ice fishing, in which a hole is made in a frozen lake, and a fishing line dangled beneath the ice, has become a favourite winter hobby in recent years.

▼ *Potatoes are important to the agricultural economy.*

Transport

Estonia has more than 56,000 km of roads and 958 km of railways. Both these networks are good, and it is easy to travel around Estonia, and to other European countries, by car or train.

▼ *The Tallinn-Pärnu-Riga highway is the main road from Estonia to the rest of Europe.*

Thanks to the support of the European Union, roads and road signs have recently been improved, and it is now easy for people to travel the short distances around the country. Over the past decade the number of Estonians owning private cars has increased, and this has seen a decrease in the use of public transport.

Public transport

Public transport in Estonia includes buses, trains, streetcars and trolleybuses, although the last two only operate in the capital, Tallinn. There is no underground rail system in Estonia, and buses are the most convenient way to travel around within the cities.

▼ *The EU has financed the many road-construction projects in Estonia, greatly improving the transport system.*

▼ *Streetcars and trolleybuses are powered by overhead electricity cables.*

Tee ehitamist rahastas Euroopa Liit
This road was built with EU support

Shipping

Estonia's shipping system is well developed, because so much of the country is bordered by the sea. There are more than 100 ports along the Baltic coast, including Tallinn, Parnu, Haapsalu and Kunda. Ferries operate between the islands and the mainland.

The largest port, the biggest train station and the international airport are all situated within Tallinn's city limits. Tallinn lies 82 km from Helsinki in Finland, 280 km from Riga in Latvia, 320 km from St Petersburg and 869 km from Moscow in Russia, 380 km from Stockholm in Sweden, and 1,045 km from Berlin in Germany.

Last winter Pille travelled to one of Estonia's islands: 'Do you know how we got there? We drove in our car across the sea on a road of ice! It was quite scary because we could see the ferry close by in the open sea, but my dad said that the ice road is really strong. We even went faster than the ferry!'

◀ From the port of Tallinn it is possible to travel to Finland, Sweden and other countries aboard a variety of vessels owned by different shipping companies.

▼ Estonia's largest international airport is in Tallinn. The national airline company is Estonian Air, which operates direct flights to many European destinations.

The economy

Since it gained independence in 1991, Estonia has been moving towards a market economy. Many industries were privatised again, and the country sought foreign investment. It became a member of the World Trade Organization in 1999 and this, together with its membership of the European Union in 2004, has helped stabilise and improve the economy.

Industry and agriculture

Estonia is a small country with no major industries, although machines, building materials, textiles, clothes, footwear and furniture are all made in the country. Approximately 22 per cent of Estonia's workforce is employed in these sectors, particularly in the timber, textile and metalworking industries. All these goods are exported to other countries.

▼ *The traditional timber industry produces lumber, furniture and other items, such as skis. Furniture manufacture is the most successful industry in Estonia.*

The number of people working in the agricultural sector is diminishing rapidly. In 1989, 18 per cent of the population worked in farming; now this number has decreased to only 6.5 per cent. This is largely because of the mechanisation of agriculture, particularly in pig-breeding and chicken-farming – fewer workers are now needed in these branches of the industry.

Milk and eggs are the most important dairy products and the major crop product is potatoes. The food-processing industry is based on local fish, meat and dairy products. Animal breeding (dairy cattle and pigs) is the main agricultural sector. Mayonnaise, ketchup, mustard, jam, canned vegetable products and juices are produced in Põltsamaa in the heart of Estonia.

In 1989, over 3 per cent of the Estonian working population worked in fisheries; nowadays the number of fishery workers has decreased to only 0.3 per cent. The most important fish harvested in the Baltic Sea are Baltic herring and sprat. Canned spicy sprats from Tallinn are popular outside Estonia.

▲ Tallegg is the largest poultry-processing company in Estonia.

Trade

The number of people employed in trade has grown since the country's independence. In 1989, almost 8 per cent of the Estonian workforce was employed in trade; today this has increased to almost 15 per cent. The key industries involved in trade with other countries are machinery production, wood products and textiles.

▲ These women are working in a fish-canning factory in Tallin. Here they make the popular export spicy sprat.

◄ There are many textile factories in Estonia's industrial cities. This one is in the capital Tallinn. Textiles make up more than 11 per cent of all exports.

▲ *Food-processing is an important industry in Estonia, particularly dairy products. This is a cheese-making factory.*

▼ *Anneke is one of the most popular chocolate bars produced by the Kalev company in Estonia. Kalev was established in 1806.*

Import and export

Estonia's main imports are machinery and equipment, and these make up around 33 per cent of all imported goods. Chemical products and textiles are also imported from abroad, along with food products and transport equipment. Estonia's main import partners are Finland, Germany, Sweden and Russia.

Major exports include machinery and tools, wood and paper products, textiles and furniture. The main countries Estonia exports to are Finland, Sweden, Germany and Latvia.

▶ *Estonia's most important exports and the percentages they represent.*

Machinery and tools
24%

Wood and paper
15.6%

Textile products
11.2%

Metal and metal products
8.6%

Furniture
7%

Foodstuffs
6.7%

Chemical products
4.9%

▼ The countries to which Estonian goods are exported.

Finland	25.7%
Sweden	15.2%
Germany	9.7%
Latvia	7.1%
United Kingdom	4.2%
Denmark	4%
Lithuania	3.8%
Norway	3.7%
The Netherlands	3.2%
Russia	2.6%

▼ The countries from which Estonia receives imported goods.

Finland	16.1%
Germany	11.3%
Sweden	8.8%
Russia	8.3%
China and Ukraine	4.3%
Japan	3.8%
Lithuania	3.5%
United States of America	3.3%
Italy	3.2%
Poland	2.9%

Energy

Ninety per cent of all Estonia's electricity is produced from the natural resource of oil shale. China and Brazil are the only other countries that use this method of creating electric power (see page 42).

▼ Oil is extracted from shale in Kohtla-Järve. Once all the oil shale available has been extracted from an area, the mining buildings are moved to a new location and the land is redeveloped.

Since the 1920s, oil has been obtained from oil shale in power plants in north-eastern Estonia. Oil shale is a natural resource that looks like yellow-brownish coarse sand. The sand contains bitumen (kerosene). By heating the sand to 500°C in an oxygen-free environment, the oil can be extracted. The sand is mined from the surface, so no deep tunnels need to be dug. Energy obtained from oil shale makes up about 60 per cent of the total energy needed, and up to 90 per cent of the energy produced in Estonia. In some power plants, the sand is burnt and directly transformed into electricity, like coal. Some 4,500 people work in the mines, and as many again work for the energy suppliers.

Oil shale is a fossil fuel, and the only one that occurs naturally in Estonia. It is therefore the only natural source of energy available to be mined. There is no oil or gas to be sourced in Estonia.

One disadvantage of having to rely so much on oil shale is that large pieces of land are needed for mining, and high levels of waste are produced in the process, which can have a negative effect on the environment. The government and energy industries do all they can to limit this damage and to recultivate the land after use.

◀ *Transport trains with huge drums wait to be loaded with oil shale.*

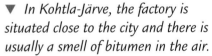

▼ *In Kohtla-Järve, the factory is situated close to the city and there is usually a smell of bitumen in the air.*

Nature

Estonia's natural habitat is richer and more diverse than that of many other countries. Old forests have not yet been cut down, wild animals still roam the forests, beaches remain unspoilt, and swamps have not been drained. Great effort is being made to maintain Estonia's natural beauty.

National parks

One of the main ways the Estonians have preserved their natural landscape is by creating national parks and nature reserves, in which the land, plants and animals are all protected by law. In these areas people are not allowed to pick plants or berries, they cannot light fires, or interfere with nature in any way. There are four national parks in Estonia, each with a great array of flora and fauna.

▲ This enormous boulder, called a 'chapel stone', is situated in northern Estonia and is a national monument. The stone is 18 metres wide and almost 7 metres high.

▼ Estonia's beaches are unspoilt by development and construction. Great care is taken to keep them clean and free of litter.

Lahemaa National Park was the first to be established in the Baltic states and is the largest in Estonia. Its name literally means 'Land of Bays' and the park is situated in northern Estonia, on the Gulf of Finland. This coastal area is covered with bays and inlets, where hundreds of stones were left behind after the last Ice Age. The stones and boulders in the Lahemaa park are all protected.

Some of the park's most beautiful features are its forests and swamps, and these are where many of the rarest plants and flowers can be found. Marshland is often covered by bog moss, which can be 3–4 metres thick in some places. In the middle of the marsh there are deep brackish waterholes or bogs. These marshes are home to many unique plants. In the Estonian countryside and national parks there are many nature trails, which lead visitors to the most unusual wildlife. Wooden planks are placed over marshes and swamps so people can get across.

The landscape in southern Estonia is protected as part of the Karula National Park. Here, numerous domes and ridges alternate with valleys and hollows, where there are swamps and lakes. In the more inaccessible areas, ancient forests survive, and these are inhabited by eagles, lynxes, wolves and bears.

▼ *Waterlogged areas like swamps and marshes cover about one-fifth of all Estonian territory.*

▼ *Sundews are one of the most interesting marsh plants because they feed on insects. Sundews capture insects that land on their leaves using the tiny hairs that grow on them. The insects cannot fly away and their bodies are absorbed by the plant. All that is left of the insects are their outer husks and wings.*

The Vilsani National Park mainly protects the offshore landscape – the sea and more than 100 islets off the coast. Hundreds of birds make their homes here, as well as the different plants and sea birds of western Estonia. Some 247 species of birds have been registered in the Vilsani National Park. The most common varieties are eiders, mallards and seagulls. Other birds, including the barnacle goose, use the park as a stopover on their migratory flights. The centre of this national park is a nineteenth-century manor house.

▲ *The hilly domes of southern Estonia are part of the Karula National Park. All the woods and swamps in this area are protected by law.*

The Soomaa National Park is situated in the middle of Estonia and was established in order to protect the swamps, meadows and forests that characterise this region – many of which have remained unchanged for centuries. In the summer, there are spectacular river floods in the national park, which cannot be seen anywhere else in Estonia.

Trees and plants

Trees, bushes and herbaceous plants have played an important role in the lives of Estonians throughout the centuries. They have provided shelter and warmth, have been used to make tools and other goods, and have been a source of food. Estonian forests, fields and meadows are home to many different species of plants, some of which are quite rare.

The forests in Estonia are mainly made up of pine and fir trees. The most common broad-leaved trees are birches, aspens and elders. Estonians regard the oak – a symbol of strength and power – as a holy tree, while maple trees are the most common trees in parks. The broadest tree in Estonia is a linden, with a girth of 9.8 metres. The tallest tree is a fir, 45 metres high; the tallest broad-leaved tree is a 40-metre aspen.

▲ *Wild boars can be seen foraging for food in woodland and boggy areas.*   ▲ *Around 4,000 beavers live in Estonia.*

Animals

There are around 80 species of mammal in Estonia. The most common are elk, roe deer, wild boars, bears, lynxes, hares, squirrels, foxes, wolves, racoons, wild dogs and hedgehogs. The lynx is the only member of the cat family living in Estonia. It is not always easy to see these animals, as they often come out in the evenings or at night, but they leave signs of their activity all over the landscape. Beavers in particular have come to be regarded as something of a pest, because the dams that they build cause flooding in the forests and meadows.

The bear is the largest predator in the country; there are believed to be around 500 bears living in the wild in Estonia. The elk is the largest animal – an adult bull can weigh up to 500 kilos. This is one of the most hunted animals in the country. Roe deer can be seen all over the forests and meadows, and they are also hunted at certain times of year. Estonia has two species of hare – grey and white; they are the fastest animals in the Estonian forests.

▼ *White storks are found all over the Estonian mainland. Here they appear on a stamp.*

Birds

Estonia is home to various forest, marsh and garden birds, as well as many species of waterfowl. The most common are the forest birds – there are 206 species of nesting birds and 38 species of migrant birds. Birds commonly found in gardens include chaffinches, thrushes, titmice, starlings, crows, magpies, sparrows and swallows.

The fields and meadows are where skylarks, lapwings, corncrakes and storks build their nests, while in the forests there are woodpeckers, nightingales, bullfinches, cuckoos, eagles and owls.

The most common waterfowl are seagulls, ducks and geese. Cranes and woodcocks live in marshes. The mute swan is the largest water bird to nest in Estonia, and their numbers have increased in recent years.

◀ *A flock of geese. Birds are protected in Estonia, and schools organise trips where the children help to 'ring' the birds — they put a small ring round one of their legs, which allows conservationists to gain information on migration and other habits.*

▼ *Signs like this are common on roadsides. It reads: 'Waste dumping forbidden!'*

Prügi mahapanek KEELATUD!

Выброс мусора ЗАПРЕЩЕН!

RMK

Environmental issues

More and more attention is being paid to environmental protection in Estonia, and the people are keen to help in any way they can. These days, recycling is common. Large waste containers are located in residential areas in towns. People sort their household waste before throwing it away so it can be easily recycled. There are four different containers – for paper, glass, hazardous waste and plastic.

As well as sorting their rubbish, other schemes are being put into place to preserve the natural environment and avoid pollution. New modern dumps are being built for all kinds of waste – large and small. Modern water processing plants are being built to provide clean and drinkable water and to prevent the rivers being polluted.

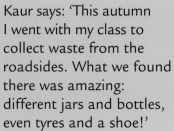

Kaur says: 'This autumn I went with my class to collect waste from the roadsides. What we found there was amazing: different jars and bottles, even tyres and a shoe!'

Taavi explains how she helped with environmental protection: 'I went to Saaremaa to clean the beach. There was a huge amount of litter. People are so stupid. They go there to sunbathe and leave their rubbish everywhere.'

Glossary

Constitution A series of laws outlining the basic principles of a government or country.

Crusades A series of military campaigns in which knights from Christian states tried to 'free' other lands from Muslim occupation.

Hanseatic League A group of German-owned towns that formed an economic and defensive unit under the control of wealthy merchants.

Middle Ages The period from around AD 500 to 1450.

Orthodox Church The Christian Church in the East, with several independent sects. In Estonia there are two main branches – Russian and Estonian Orthodox.

Paganism An ancient religion, in which followers worship several different gods. Pagan customs and beliefs vary between different groups of people.

Serfdom A social system in which labourers (serfs) were bound to a particular area of land owned by a landlord. Serfs were not slaves because they could not be sold.

Index